WORLD OF INSECTS

Termites

by Martha E. H. Rustad

BELLWETHER MEDIA • MINNEAPOLIS, MN

Note to Librarians, Teachers, and Parents:

Blastoff! Readers are carefully developed by literacy experts and combine standards-based content with developmentally-appropriate text.

Level 1 provides the most support through repetition of high-frequency words, light text, predictable sentence patterns, and strong visual support.

Level 2 offers early readers a bit more challenge through varied simple sentences, increased text load, and less repetition of high frequency words.

Level 3 advances early-fluent readers toward fluency through increased text and concept load, less reliance on visuals, longer sentences, and more literary language.

Level 4 builds reading stamina by providing more text per page, increased use of punctuation, greater variation in sentence patterns, and increasingly challenging vocabulary.

Level 5 encourages children to move from "learning to read" to "reading to learn" by providing even more text, varied writing styles, and less familiar topics.

Whichever book is right for your reader, Blastoff! Readers are the perfect books to build confidence and encourage a love of reading that will last a lifetime!

This edition first published in 2008 by Bellwether Media.

No part of this publication may be reproduced in whole or in part without written permission of the publisher. For information regarding permission, write to Bellwether Media Inc., Attention: Permissions Department, Post Office Box 1C, Minnetonka, MN 55345-9998.

Library of Congress Cataloging-in-Publication Data
Rustad, Martha E. H. (Martha Elizabeth Hillman), 1975–
    Termites / by Martha E.H. Rustad.
        p. cm. – (Blastoff! readers. World of insects)
    Summary: "Simple text accompanied by full-color photographs give an upclose look at termites. Intended for kindergarten through third grade students"—Provided by publisher.
    Includes bibliographical references and index.
    ISBN-13: 978-1-60014-108-9 (hardcover : alk. paper)
    ISBN-10: 1-60014-108-0 (hardcover : alk. paper)
    1. Termites—Juvenile literature. I. Title.

QL529.R87 2008
595.7'36–dc22   2007009766

Contents

What Are Termites?   4

Termite Colonies   5

Termite Jobs   6

Termite Nests   12

Termites and Wood   18

Glossary   22

To Learn More   23

Index   24

Termites are **insects**.
Their soft bodies are white
or brown.

Termites live in groups called **colonies**. Millions of termites may live in one colony.

All termites have jobs. Some start new colonies. They are called **kings** and **queens**.

6

One king and one queen start
each colony. Only king and
queen termites have wings.

A king and queen fly to find a place for their colony. Then their wings fall off.

The queen makes eggs in her body to start the colony. Her body grows very big!

Some termites are **soldiers**. They guard the colony from **enemies** such as ants.

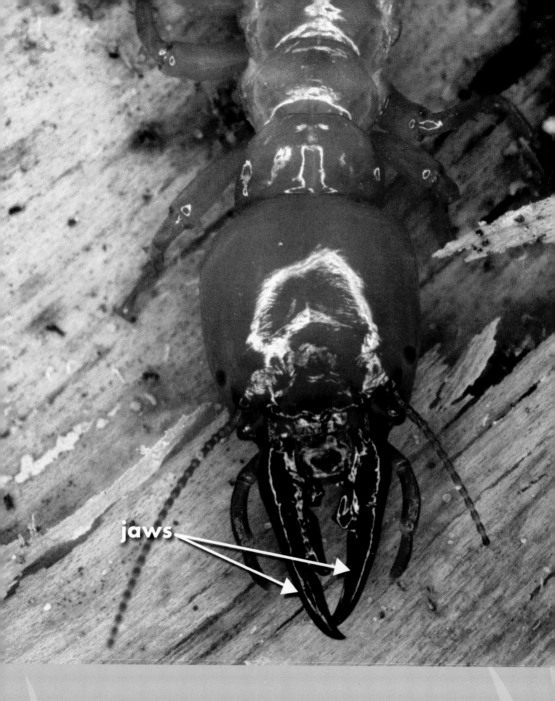

jaws

They have big heads and
jaws for fighting enemies.

Some termites are **workers**.
They build the colony's nest.

Termites build nests in dirt or wood.

Termites dig many tunnels and rooms in their nest.

Some termites build dirt **mounds** above the ground.

15

Termites spend most of their time in the dark. Some don't even have eyes.

antennas

Termites have two straight **antennas**. Termites use their antennas to feel and smell.

17

Termites eat plants and wood. They have strong jaws for chewing.

18

Some termites chew through wooden homes and furniture.

Termites break down dead
trees into fresh dirt.

Fresh dirt helps new
plants grow.

Glossary

antennas—a pair of thin feelers on an insect's head

colony—a large group of insects that live together

enemies—ones that want to harm another; termite enemies include anteaters and ants.

insect—a kind of animal with six legs; most insects also have a hard body, two antennas, and two or four wings.

king—a male termite that can produce young with the queen; each colony has one king.

mound—a hill or pile

queen—a female termite that lays eggs; each colony has one queen; queen termites grow to be much larger than other termites.

soldier—a kind of termite that keeps the nest safe

worker—a termite that builds the nest

To Learn More

AT THE LIBRARY

Green, Jen. *Termites*. Danbury, Conn.: Grolier, 2004.

Hartley, Karen, Chris Macro, and Philip Taylor. *Termite*. Chicago, Ill.: Heinemann Library, 2006.

Hirschmann, Kris. *Termite*. San Diego, Calif.: KidHaven Press, 2006.

Schuh, Mari C. *Termites*. Mankato, Minn.: Capstone Press, 2003.

ON THE WEB
Learning more about termites is as easy as 1, 2, 3.

1. Go to www.factsurfer.com

2. Enter "termites" into search box.

3. Click the "Surf" button and you will see a list of related web sites.

With factsurfer.com, finding more information is just a click away.

Index

antennas, 17

ants, 10

bodies, 4, 9

colonies, 5, 6, 7, 8, 9,
   10, 12

dark, 16

dirt, 13, 15, 20, 21

eggs, 9

enemies, 10, 11

eyes, 16

furniture, 19

ground, 15

groups, 5

heads, 11

homes, 19

insects, 4

jaws, 11, 18

jobs, 6

king, 6, 7, 8

mounds, 15

nest, 12, 13, 14

plants, 18, 21

rooms, 14

queen, 6, 7, 8, 9

soldiers, 10

trees, 20

tunnels, 14

wings, 7, 8

wood, 13, 18

workers, 12

The photographs in this book are reproduced through the courtesy of: George Grall/Getty Images, front cover, p. 10, 13, 17; Terry Whittaker/Alamy, p. 4; jeridu, pp. 5, 8-9, 12, 20; Peggy Easterly, pp. 6-7; Andy Williams/CritterZone.com, pp. 11, 18; Bryan Mullennix/Getty Images, p. 14; Craig Ruaux, p. 15; Holt Studios International Ltd/Alamy, p. 16; Bartomeu Borrell, p. 19; Kanwarjit Singh Boparal, p. 21.